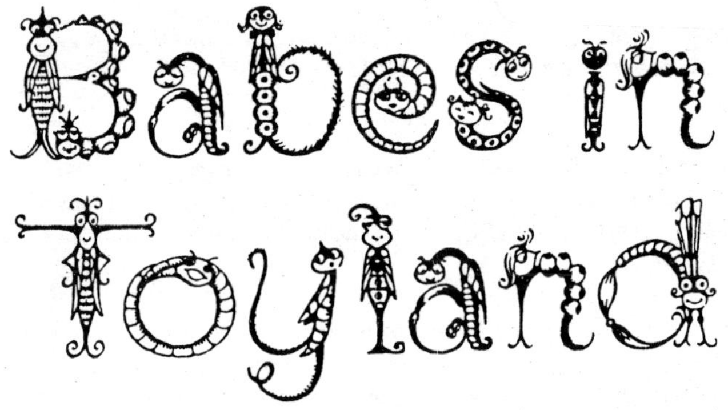

Book and Lyrics by

R. EUGENE JACKSON

Based on Glen MacDonough's Original Play

Music by

Victor Herbert

Adapted and Arranged by

Carl Alette

I. E. CLARK PUBLICATIONS
PO Box 246, Schulenburg, TX 78956-0246
Phone (979)743-3232 ** FAX (979)743-4765
E-mail: ieclark@cvtv.net

ISBN 0-88680-267-9

BABES IN TOYLAND

Characters

Uncle Barnaby, a rich miser in love with Mistress Mary
Alan, Barnaby's nephew, also in love with Mistress Mary
Mistress Mary Quite Contrary, in love with Alan
The Widow Piper, Mistress Mary's mother
Gonzorgo, a hard-hearted ruffian
Roderigo, his soft-hearted partner
Gypsies (as many as desired)†
The Giant Spider

CHORUS (Characters of Mother Goose Land)†

***Simple Simon**
***Jack**
***Jill**
***Little Bo Peep**
***Little Miss Muffet**
***Peter Peter Pumpkin Eater**
Little Tommy Tucker
***Little Boy Blue**
Bobbie Shaftoe
Sallie Waters
***Tom Tom the Piper's Son**
***Mary Had a Little Lamb**
***Jack Be Nimble**
Queen of Hearts
Attendant to the Queen of Hearts
Humpty Dumpty
Three Blind Mice
Three Men in a Tub
Little Jack Horner
(More or fewer Mother Goose characters may be used)
**Speaking roles*

Characters in Toyland

The Toymaster
Grumio, apprentice in the Toymaster's workshop
Inspector Marmaduke, of the Toyland Police
Toys that come to life (Soldiers, Dolls, Robots, and others)†
†Mother Goose Chorus may double as Gypsies and Toys

•

TIME: Somewhere in the imagination

PLACE: Act I, Scene 1: Mother Goose Land
Act I, Scene 2: The Spider's Forest
Act II: Toyland

First produced by Theatre USA at the University of South Alabama in 12 performances, Dec. 8-12, 1986.

ABOUT THE PLAY

Critics loved Victor Herbert's music when BABES IN TOYLAND was first produced in New York in 1903. But they were rather cool to the book with its confusing storyline full of puns which children would not understand.

The beautiful, memorable music and the Mother Goose characters have made BABES IN TOYLAND a perennial theatre favorite. But few if any of the several adaptations were an improvement on the original plot. That's why we asked Gene Jackson, one of America's most popular authors of plays for children's theatre, to rework the story and to update and clarify the lyrics for today's children.

Jackson eliminated some of the extraneous and confusing minor characters while strengthening the major characters into three-dimensional roles that become a joy for actors and audiences alike. "We maintained the basic original story while rewriting the dialog completely," Jackson said.

A 1959 Walt Disney movie based on the operetta starred Ray Bolger as the evil Barnaby, Tommy Sands and Annette Funicello as Alan and Mistress Mary, and Ed Wynn as the Master Toymaker.

The play begins with Mother Goose characters–as many or as few as the director wants to use–all astir over the rivalry between handsome young Alan and his miserly, mean-hearted Uncle Barnaby for the love of Mistress Mary Quite Contrary. The latest news is that Alan has disappeared. Uncle Barnaby enters the scene to announce that Alan has drowned. Two ruffians, Gonzorgo and Roderigo, confirm the tragedy; they were on the boat when it sank.

Barnaby is ecstatic. Now no one stands in the way of his courtship of Mary, and–even more important–he will inherit his nephew's fortune. It's not hard to guess that Barnaby arranged Alan's "accident" through the two evil but clownish hit men. So inept are Roderigo and Gonzorgo that Alan turns up unharmed–the boat "sank" in two feet of water. But Barnaby is determined to get his way.

To avoid his evil clutches, Alan and Mary try to escape to Toyland. But the dangerous Spider's Forest lies in the way, and the Spider nearly has Mary trapped in the web when Alan rescues her. They get to Toyland, but even there they are not safe, for Barnaby and his two thugs have followed them. The villains find a machine recently invented by the Master Toymaker which will bring dolls to life. By switching the wires, Barnaby believes the machine will turn the dolls into killer robots. In colorful costumes and to the stirring music of "The March of the Toys," the dolls attack . . . whom? Barnaby and his henchmen—or Alan and Mary? The action and suspense continue right up to the exciting climax.

Jackson has given the characters three-dimensional personalities. Mary is often contrary; but she can be loving and gentle, too. Barnaby's heart is full of avarice and disdain for humanity, but he truly loves Mary. And so on through the *dramatis personae.*

Although the play starts with a Christmas tree, it is not really a Christmas story; it is suitable for any season of the year. The author has written alternate lyrics for the opening song for a non-Christmas production —see page 41.

Playing time: 75 minutes

Barnaby proposing to Mistress Mary Quite Contrary (Theatre U. S. A.)

Musical Numbers

No. 1: Overture

ACT I, Scene 1

No. 2: "Hail to Christmas" (Chorus of Mother Goose characters)
No. 3A: "Gypsy Music" (Gypsies dance or cavort)
No. 3B: "Floretta" (Alan, Gypsy Chorus)
No. 4A: "Sad Music" (under dialog)
No. 4B: "I Can't Do the Sum" (Mary, Mother Goose Chorus)
No. 5: "He Won't Be Happy Till He Gets It" (Barnaby, Gonzorgo, Roderigo)
No. 6A: "He Won't Be Happy Till He Gets It" reprise (Gonzorgo, Roderigo)
No. 6B: "Scene Change Music"
No. 6C: "Mysterious Music"

ACT I, Scene 2

No. 7: "Go To Sleep, Slumber Deep" (Mary, Alan)
No. 8: "Act I Finale"

ACT II

No. 9: "Opening Scene Music"
No. 10: "Toyland" (Toymaster, Toy Chorus)
No. 11: "He Won't Be Happy Till He Gets It" reprise (Barnaby, Gonzorgo, Roderigo, Marmaduke)
No. 12: "March of the Toys" (Toy Chorus parade)
No. 13A: Intro to "Toyland" for curtain calls
No. 13B: "Toyland" (the Company)
No. 13C: "He Won't Be Happy Till He Gets It" (Marmaduke, Barnaby, Gonzorgo, Roderigo)
No. 13D: "Toyland" (the Company)

Available from the Publisher:

Piano/Vocal Score

Demonstration/Accompaniment Tape. Side A has vocals and music. Side B has music only, professionally played by an orchestra—for use as accompaniment at rehearsals and for performances, if desired. Available on cassette or reel-to-reel tape.

Video Cassette Tape of a live performance by a university theatre.

BABES IN TOYLAND

ACT I

Music No. 1: "OVERTURE"

Scene 1

[A street in Mother Goose Land. Each house or area should represent some familiar scene from a Mother Goose rhyme. For example, one house should be a big old shoe; another should be a large pumpkin.

The characters are likewise from Mother Goose Land and should dress according to the traditional view of them.

AT RISE: *The MOTHER GOOSE CHARACTERS carry in a large Christmas tree, set it Up Center. They sing as they enter and decorate the tree. (See p. 41 for non-Christmas presentation)]*

Music No. 2: "HAIL TO CHRISTMAS"

CHORUS. Hail to Christmas, joyous Christmas!
Hooray! The day draws near;
Hail to Christmas, joyous Christmas!
Be happy, it's almost here.

Santa Claus may bring a full sleigh
And here unload his haul;
Santa Claus will make us each thrill
Because he has toys for all.

SOLO. Folks come from Toyland
And from far, far and near;
Folks come to join us–
And to share our holiday cheer.

CHORUS. To our fair; to our fair–
They come from miles around for fun and games
At our fair.

Santa Claus may bring a full sleigh
And here unload his haul;
Santa Claus will make us each thrill
Because he has toys for all!

[MISTRESS MARY makes a grand entrance]

CHORUS. *[Ad-libbed]* Look, it's Mistress Mary, Quite Contrary! / Hello, Mary. / Mary, you look beautiful. / How does your garden grow,

Mistress Mary? *[MARY sadly hangs her head]* What is it, Mary? / Why so sad? / What a happy day! / Christmas is near!

MARY. This would be such a happy occasion if only Alan were here. Has anyone seen him?

CHORUS. *[Ad-libbed]* No, Mistress Mary. / Not I. / I haven't. / Sorry.

MARY. I'm going over to his house to look one more time. Good-bye. *[She exits]*

CHORUS. *[Ad-libbed]* Good-bye. / So long. / See you later.

JACK. *[Who wears a bandage around his head and carries a pail with JILL]* Why do you suppose Mistress Mary is so concerned . . .?

JILL. About finding Alan?

BO PEEP. *[Who carries a staff]* Because they're in love, sillies.

MISS MUFFET. *[Who carries a bowl of curds and whey along with a large spoon]* But Alan has been missing for almost a week. It's very strange.

MARY HAD A LITTLE LAMB. *[She pulls a lamb on a small wagon]* How sad! Does anyone know where he is? Tom Tom, the piper's son, did you see him while you were running away?

TOM TOM THE PIPER'S SON. *[He carries a pig under his arm]* No. No one has seen him since the Mother Goose County Fair several days ago.

BARNABY. *[Enters furtively. He is a villain in every sense of the word. He wears a black suit, a cape, and a black top hat. He is followed by GONZORGO, a nasty ruffian, and RODERIGO, a sentimental pal. BARNABY bellows]* Well, hello, everyone! *[The OTHERS, caught off guard, scream and back off. They compose themselves after seeing him. He delights in his evil ways]* Tee-hee, I didn't . . . frighten you . . . did I? Tee-hee-hee.

LITTLE BOY BLUE. *[Who is dressed in blue and carries a bugle. He is scared]* W-w-who, us? Never.

OTHERS. *[Ad-libbed]* N-n-never! / No! / Not us!

BARNABY. Are you enjoying this little party I planned? Hmmmm?

JACK. This is *your* party?

JILL. *Your* tree and *your* punch?

BARNABY. Of course. Tee-hee-hee. Who did you think was paying for it?

BO PEEP. I don't believe it. Only yesterday you cleaned out Old Mother Hubbard's cupboard because she couldn't pay her rent. And now her poor dog doesn't even have a bone to gnaw on.

MARY HAD A LITTLE LAMB. And the day before, you forced Jack Be Nimble to jump over a candlestick.

JACK BE NIMBLE. Yeah. But I slipped and fell, and my pants caught on fire! *[He turns his back so that a big burned spot can be seen on his backside]*

BARNABY. It's true. Tee-hee-hee. *[With a swagger and a big smile]* And tomorrow I may chase the three blind mice and cut off their tails with a carving knife. Tee-hee-hee. *[The THREE BLIND MICE squeal and hide behind the others]* But I've thrown this party as a celebration.

OTHERS. *[Ad-libbed]* A celebration? / Of what? / What is it? / What are you celebrating?

BARNABY. I've decided to enter the heavenly state of matrimony.

TOM TOM THE PIPER'S SON. You're what?

BARNABY. *[Plainly]* I'm getting married.

MISS MUFFET. Who's the unlucky girl?

BARNABY. *[Proudly]* Mistress Mary, Quite Contrary. Tee-hee-hee.

LITTLE BOY BLUE. What? You can't do that.

SIMPLE SIMON. She's in love with your nephew, Alan.

BARNABY. *[Slyly]* Tee-hee-hee. Perhaps she *was* in love with him. Sad to say, poor Alan has gone to that Great Toyland in the Sky.

TOM TOM THE PIPER'S SON. He's where?

BARNABY. Dead.

JACK. No.

BARNABY. Yes.

JILL. Can't be.

BARNABY. Is. He drowned when a ship he was on unexpectedly sank.

MISS MUFFET. We don't believe you.

BARNABY. If you don't believe me, perhaps you will take it from these two, uh, gentlemen. This is Gonzorgo, captain of the ship.

GONZORGO. *[He growls his words]* It's true, lass. After the Mother Goose County Fair, he insisted we take him for a ride on our boat, The Leaky Bucket.

BARNABY. And this is Roderigo, the crew of the ship.

RODERIGO. *[Weeping in a giant handkerchief]* A big storm came *up,* and The Leaky Bucket went *down.*

GONZORGO. We were the only survivors.

RODERIGO. Everybody else is at the bottom of the sea. *[He cries louder]* With all the little fishes!

BARNABY. *[Feigning concern]* I'm terribly broken-hearted.

BO PEEP. *[To Barnaby]* And what is his broken-hearted Uncle Barnaby going to do with Alan's fortune?

BARNABY. Why, keep it, of course. I'm sure that's what he would want me to do. Tee-hee-hee. I've even bought a new mansion up on the hill–for Mistress Mary and me. *[He laughs]*

SIMPLE SIMON. You skinflint! We don't believe a word you say.

BARNABY. Enjoy the goodies, friends. Think of it as a Christmas gala and my engagement party. Tee-hee-hee. *[Pause as the others react]* Please. When you see lovely Mistress Mary, tell her I'm waiting for her with baited breath. *[He pants heavily]*

JACK. Excuse us. We've got to go up the hill . . .

JILL. To fetch a pail of water.

TOM TOM THE PIPER'S SON. And I've got to find another pig and run away..

BO PEEP. And I've got to look for my lost sheep, even though I don't know where to find them. *[The CROWD rushes off, leaving BARNABY, GONZORGO, and RODERIGO alone]*

BARNABY. *[All smiles]* Excellent work, you ugly ruffians. Now, tell me how you did the dastardly deed.

GONZORGO. *[As mean and nasty as possible]* First, we saw Alan at the Fair, just like you said. Then we lured him down to the dock.

RODERIGO. *[As he weeps]* Where we–where we threw a nasty bag over him and dragged him on board a broken down old tub of a ship.

GONZORGO. A storm came up as we set sail. So we jumped ship and left Alan to his fate.

RODERIGO. The boat had so many cracks and holes in it, it started sinking right away.

GONZORGO. We made it back to land safely, but he didn't. Tsk, tsk, tsk. *[He chuckles gruffly]*

RODERIGO. And now he's floating around–with all the little fishes! *[He sobs loudly. BARNABY cries lightly]*

GONZORGO. Why are you crying?

BARNABY. Because I've seen the last of my little charge, Alan.

GONZORGO. And here's the first of our little charges– *[He hands him a slip of paper]* Our bill.

RODERIGO. *Our* little charge for getting rid of *your* little charge.

BARNABY. *[He reads it and is shocked]* A thousand dollars?!

GONZORGO. We had to risk our lives, matey.

BARNABY. Very well. I don't carry anthing larger than a quarter with me, so you'll have to meet me here later in the day. I'll pay you then.

GONZORGO. Aye, we'll be here. But don't keep us waitin'.

RODERIGO. *[Wiping his eyes with his handkerchief]* Yeah, we get very mean when we're kept waitin', don't we, Gonzorgo?

GONZORGO. Yeah, mean. *[He growls]*

BARNABY. Yes, yes, all right. *[He brightens]* But right now, I've got to prepare for my. . . proposal of marriage. Tee-hee-hee. *[He exits laughing evilly]*

GONZORGO. An odd sort, isn't he?

RODERIGO. A villain, if you ask me. *[They exit]*

[The CROWD enters escorting MISTRESS MARY]

MARY. He still wasn't home. I have no idea where Alan could be.

JACK. *[As MARY crosses Center]* I'm afraid we know where he is, Mistress Mary.

JILL. Old man Barnaby told us.

MARY. *[Excited]* Really? You've found him? *[She looks around; contrarily]* Well, where is he?

BO PEEP. Drowned.

MARY. *[Shocked]* Drowned? My sweet Alan is . . . gone?

TOM TOM THE PIPER'S SON. His ship sank–with him on it.

SIMPLE SIMON. We're very sorry, Mistress Mary.

MARY. It can't be. *[She cries]* It can't be! *[She exits into her house]*

HUMPTY DUMPTY. *[Sadly]* All the king's horses and all the king's men couldn't bring him back again.

LITTLE BOY BLUE. Even the great Toymaker of Toyland couldn't help him now. *[They begin to exit]*

JACK BE NIMBLE. I feel sorry for poor Mistress Mary, even though she is quite contrary.

BO PEEP. Yes. But her garden does grow very well.

CHORUS. *[Ad-libbed]* Yes, it does. / Oh, it's a great garden. / The best. / Poor Mistress Mary.

[They exit in various directions as BARNABY enters holding a bouquet of flowers with a note attached]

BARNABY. Mistress Mary wasn't in her garden. Perhaps she's in her house. *[He sings out]* Mistress Mary? Oh, Mistress Mary? It is I, your husband-to-be. Tee-hee-hee.

Music No. 3A: "GYPSY MUSIC" (for ALAN's entrance)

[ALAN enters dressed as a gypsy woman. He is accompanied by GYPSIES playing tambourines, clanging their handbells, and having a good time. ALAN sees Barnaby. The MUSIC stops. He speaks to the other Gypsies]

ALAN. Ah-ha! It's old Uncle Barnaby. I'll have a little fun with him. *[He dances to him and disguises his voice]* Hello, big man.

BARNABY. What? Oh, a gypsy woman. Go away. I'm waiting for my bride-to-be.

ALAN. Oh? Is she giving you a little trouble? Perhaps I can help.

Music No. 3B: "FLORETTA"

[Throughout the song, BARNABY tries to ignore him, but ALAN persists]

ALAN. Great are my magical charms,
Like casting a spell over someone;
I'm also a voodoo at casting a hoodoo,
Especially if she's a dumb one.

Floretta, Floretta the gypsy am I.
I'll tell you the future I see in your eye,
And I'll read your fortune from your palm at a glance.
Please notice I also collect in advance.

GYPSIES/CHORUS. *[The GYPSIES may sing the following, or the CHORUS may enter and add to the singing]*
Floretta, Floretta the gypsy is she.
Far into the future your fate she can see,

ALAN/GYPSIES/CHORUS. And (I'll/she'll) tell your fortune from your palm at a glance.
Please notice, (I/she) also collect(s) in advance.

ALAN. Are you unhappy in love?
And does she presume to ignore you?
I'll give you a session to teach her a lesson
And cause her to madly adore you.

Floretta, Floretta the gypsy am I.
I'll tell you the future I see in your eye,
And I'll read your fortune from your palm at a glance.
Please notice, I also collect in advance.

GYPSIES/CHORUS. Floretta, Floretta the gypsy is she.
Far into the future your fate she can see;
ALAN/GYPSIES/CHORUS. And (I'll/she'll) tell your fortune from your palm at a glance.
Please notice, (I/she) also collect(s) in advance.

[At the end, ALAN's headpiece comes off and BARNABY recognizes him. If the CHORUS is used, they now exit, having failed to recognize Alan]

BARNABY. Alan! You . . . but . . . you're supposed to be fish food. I should know. I gave the orders . . . uh, I mean, I heard it from some seamen.

ALAN. As you can see, Uncle Barnaby, I'm alive and well.

BARNABY. Alive and well. Well, well . . . well, uh, how . . . nice.

ALAN. And I want my inheritance that you have been keeping for me. The one my parents left for me.

BARNABY. Huh? Well, uh, why all the rush? Can't I keep it just a little longer? Hmmmm?

ALAN. No. I'm planning to wed Mistress Mary.

BARNABY. *[He flinches, but composes himself]* Arghhh! I see. Very well. Tee-hee-hee, since you've been gone, however, I have moved to a mansion at a distance from here. At noon, I'll send two men to meet you here. They will, uh, escort you . . . to my new home. *[He chuckles fiendishly]*

ALAN. I'll be here with bells on.

BARNABY. Good. But I'd take the dress off, if I were you.

ALAN. What? Oh, this old thing. My clothes were ripped and these gypsies were kind enough to lend me this. Uh, it was all they had.

BARNABY. Yes, I see.

ALAN. I'll go and change right now. Come on, gypsies. *[They start off]*

BARNABY. By the way, Alan. *[ALAN turns back to him]* You can forget about Mistress Mary. She has agreed to accept *my* hand in marriage. Tee-hee-hee.

ALAN. What? *[Crosses after him]* But that's impossible. She's in love with me. I can't believe it.

BARNABY. Believe what you like. I am just now on my way to make my proposal official. Good day, my dear nephew.

ALAN. I won't believe it. I won't. Unless I see some proof. *[He exits with the GYPSIES]*

BARNABY. *[Calling out musically]* Mistress Ma-a-ary? Mistress Ma-a-a-ary? *[No answer. He stomps up to her house angrily. As he starts to bang on the door, MARY opens it. The force of his swing carries him into the house. MARY steps outside and watches him going inside]* Oooowwwwwwww! *[There is a loud crash]*

MARY. Oh!

BARNABY. *[Comes back to the doorway. He is disheveled but tries to smile through his pain]* Ooh, that hurts! *[He sees Mary and pulls himself together]* Well, my dear Mistress Mary. I brought these for you. *[He holds up the bouquet of flowers, which is now smashed and broken]*

MARY. But why would you want to give me a bouquet of broken flowers? *[She takes them]*

BARNABY. Broken flowers? *[He looks at them]* Oh. Well, they weren't broken when I arrived here. *[He tries to straighten them]* There. Good as new. Well, almost.

MARY. But why me?

BARNABY. Why you? Well, Mistress Mary. I wish to speak to you about something very personal. Won't you step into my house?

MARY. That's my house.

BARNABY. Your house? Oh, yes, indeed. My mistake. *[He pulls her to a bench]* Uh, won't you step over here to this bench that I donated to Mother Goose County? Yes, there we are. *[He still hurts but he sits close to her. She inches away. He speaks as if the lines are memorized]* I hope that you will accept these flowers . . . *[He moves closer to her. She moves away]* As a token of . . . *[He moves closer. She stands and moves off]* My lov . . . owwwwww! *[As he tries to move closer, he falls off the edge of the bench]*

MARY. What are you doing down there?

BARNABY. I'm on my. . . *[pulls himself to his knees and takes her hand]* knees . . . so that I may propose to you, Mistress Mary.

MARY. Propose? What do you propose?

BARNABY. *[Gets angry]* What do I propose? What does a man propose to a woman when he's on his knees? He proposes marriage. I've decided to let you marry me.

MARY. Marry you? Me? Really?

BARNABY. Why not? I'll be rich as soon as I get Alan's inheritance. I'm certainly a handsome fellow. And a nicer guy you'll never meet.

MARY. But, sir, you're old enough to be my father.

BARNABY. Well, maybe.

MARY. You're even old enough to be my grandfather.

BARNABY. Well, may... What?! Your *grand*father? Never! Besides, what does it matter? There are many young ladies in Mother Goose County who would be happy to have me as a husband.

MARY. Then, sir, I suggest you propose to them. My heart belonged to Alan. And now that he's gone, I . . . *[She cries]*

BARNABY. But, but . . . I've even written a poem for you. Listen. *[He reads from the card attached to the flowers, almost jerking them out of Mary's hands]* "Mistress Mary, quite contrary,
How does your garden grow?
With cockle shells and silver bells
And thousand dollar bills all in a row."
Do you like it?

MARY. Well, it's . . . unique.

BARNABY. The message continues, "Will you marry me, Mistress Mary?" I even wrote in the answer for you. "Yes, I would love to marry you, Barnaby, and that will entitle you to all my possessions and money." And I signed it, "Love, Mistress Mary."

MARY. Sir, I resent your attitude, and I resent you. I wouldn't marry you if you were the last man in the County. *[She turns away and folds her arms across her chest]*

BARNABY. Ahhh, well, I think that can be arranged. Hmmmm. *[He brightens and exits calling]* Oh, Captain Gonzorgo? Roderigo? I have a little job for you.

MARY. I wonder what he meant by that? *[She hears laughing and cheering from the CHORUS]* Now, what is that all about? *[Some CHORUS MEMBERS enter, pushing ALAN ahead of them. He is now properly dressed. When they see Mary, the CHORUS backs off, smiling. ALAN pauses. MARY is shocked]* Alan? Alan is that you?

ALAN. None other.

MARY. *[She rushes toward him]* Oh, Alan, I was told you drowned. But you're not drowned at all. You're . . . you're not even wet. *[She takes his hands]*

ALAN. That's right, Mistress Mary. I was abducted by two bumbling scalawags. They bound and gagged me and hauled me aboard a schooner. A slight rain came up, the ship began to sink, and they jumped overboard.

MARY. But how did you escape if you were tied up?

ALAN. When I finally broke loose and got out of the bag, I discovered that we had never left the dock. The ship had sunk tied up to it.

MARY. But, if you went down with the ship . . . ?

ALAN. Dearest Mary, the water was only a few feet deep at the dock. I never even got my feet wet–no thanks to those two villains who kidnapped me. But I still don't understand what they had against me.

MARY. That doesn't matter, now, Alan–now that you're safe and sound.

ALAN. You're as lovely as ever, Mistress Mary.

MARY. Why, thank you.

ALAN. *[Sees the flowers on the ground]* Oh, look. What's this? *[He picks them up]*

MARY. Leave them there, Alan. They're no good.

ALAN. Aren't these the flowers Uncle Barnaby was carrying?

MARY. Who cares? *[She tries to pull them away]* Let's talk about other things.

ALAN. No, wait. There's a note attached.

MARY. A note? *[She remembers what it says]* I'm sure it's nothing –really. *[She tries again to pull them away]* Alan!

ALAN. *[He looks at her severely]* So that's why you don't want me to read the card. It's from my Uncle Barnaby. *[He reads it]* "Will you marry me, Mistress Mary?" *[He looks at her]* And there's a response from you.

MARY. Let me explain, Alan. It isn't what it seems.

ALAN. *[Reading]* "Yes, I would love to marry you, Barnaby, and that will entitle you to all my possessions and money." And it's signed, "Love, Mistress Mary." *[He looks at her accusingly]* What does this mean?

MARY. It's a mistake, that's all. If you'd just let me–

ALAN. It's a mistake, all right–and I made it. I was in love with you. I thought you were in love with me. Uncle Barnaby told me you had agreed to marry him, but I told him I wouldn't believe it unless I saw some proof. *[He waves the card in her face]* Well, now, I've seen it. Good-bye, Mistress Mary. Good-bye forever! *[He pushes the flowers into her hands and stalks off. MARY chases him a few paces before she pauses]*

Music No. 4A: "SAD MUSIC" (under)

MARY. Well, if that's what you think of my love, Alan, good-bye to you, too! *[She begins to cry. After a few seconds, she composes herself]*

Well, maybe I *should* marry Barnaby! At least he trusts me. *[The MUSIC fades out as the CHORUS rushes on. They carry schoolbooks and slates and chalk]*

BO PEEP. Mistress Mary, you've got to help us. I'm so bad at mathematics, I can't even count my lost sheep.

MISS MUFFET. And I don't even remember how many bowls of curds and whey I've eaten.

JACK. So how can we pass math class . . .

JILL. If we can't do the simplest problems?

LITTLE BOY BLUE. But you were always very good with numbers.

JACK BE NIMBLE. So, will you help us with our homework?

MARY. Please, children, not now.

BO PEEP. It's got to be now, Mistress Mary. We don't have any other time.

MISS MUFFET. Won't you just look at it? Teacher says if anybody can do it, you can. *[She pushes a book into Mary's hands]*

MARY. I'm really not in the mood.

CHORUS. Please, Mistress Mary?

MARY. *[She is defeated. She opens the book]* Well, I'll *look* at it.

Music No. 4B: "I CAN'T DO THE SUM"

MARY. *[Reads]* If a steamship weighed ten thousand tons,
And sailed five thousand miles
With a cargo full of teddy bears
And dolls with great big smiles;
If the men were almost six feet tall
And the captain near the same,
Would you subtract or multiply
To find the captain's name?

[She puts down the book and picks up a slate]

CHORUS. Oh, oh, oh.

MARY. Put down six and carry two; *[She writes on her slate in rhythm]*

CHORUS. *[They write on their slates in rhythm]* Put down six; carry two.

MARY. Gee, but this is hard to do;

CHORUS. Yes, it is–hard to do.

MARY. I don't care what teacher says,
I can't do the sum. *[She erases it, then opens the book again and reads]*

If Harold took sweet Imogene
With him one night to dine;
She ordered everything in sight
With lots and lots of wine;
If one hundred dollars was the cost,
But he had just thirty-four,
How many things would Harold strike,
Before he struck the floor?

[She puts the book down and picks up the slate]

CHORUS. Oh, oh, oh.

MARY. *[She writes on her slate in rhythm]* Put down five and carry nine;

CHORUS. *[They write on their slates in rhythm]* Put down five; carry nine.

MARY.. I don't know what you will find;

CHORUS. We don't know–what we'll find.

MARY/CHORUS. You can think and think and think
til you say. . .

MARY. "Ho-hum."

MARY/CHORUS. I don't care what teacher says,

MARY. I can't do the sum;

CHORUS. You can't do the sum?
How glum!

MARY/CHORUS. (I/we) can't do the sum.

[After the song, MARY begins to weep]

MARY HAD A LITTLE LAMB. Mistress Mary, what is it? You look as sad as a little lamb.

MARY. I'm sorry. I can't seem to hold my tears back.

BO PEEP. Can we help you?

MARY. *[Sniffing and drying her eyes]* I'm afraid not, my friends. But thank you for the offer.

MISS MUFFET. It's that old Barnaby, isn't it? Is he still demanding that you marry him?

BO PEEP. Even though Alan has returned?

MARY. Yes.

LITTLE BOY BLUE. But with Alan here you should be smiling, not crying.

MARY. Except that he doesn't trust me any more. *[She cries. The CHORUS sympathizes with her. Finally, she rises with renewed confi-*

dence] That settles it. I'm leaving. I'm going away, and I'm never coming back. *[She starts toward her house]*

SIMPLE SIMON. Where will you go?

MARY. I don't know. But I really should have some destination, shouldn't I? *[Pause]* I know. I'll go to Toyland. They're always in need of help there. I'm sure I can get a job with the Great Toymaker.

WIDOW PIPER. *[A matronly type, she enters from Mary's house]* Mistress Mary, Quite Contrary, what is going on out here?

MARY. It's all my friends, Mother Piper. They're wishing me a fond farewell.

WIDOW PIPER. You're going somewhere?

MARY. *[As she begins to cry]* I'll explain later. *[She rushes into the house]*

WIDOW PIPER. Well, I never! Will somebody please explain?

JACK. Later, Widow Piper. We've got to get back to school.

JILL. Good-bye. Good-bye. *[The CHORUS exits. The WIDOW PIPER looks around, surprised at their sudden exit]*

WIDOW PIPER. What's the matter? Do I smell like a dead fish or something?

BARNABY. *[Enters, sees her, and crosses to her]* Widow Piper, may I have a word with you? Hmmmm?

WIDOW PIPER. Why, Barnaby, you old good-for-nothing. What do you want from me? *[She preens]*

BARNABY. Madam, I wish to speak to you about a certain marriage.

WIDOW PIPER. *[Thinking he is speaking of marrying her]* Marriage? Why, Barnaby, the least you could have done is warn me so I could have worn my Sunday best.

BARNABY. As you know, I have a lot to offer a woman.

WIDOW PIPER. You do?

BARNABY. Yes. Such as a charming personality. *[He flutters his eyelids]*

WIDOW PIPER. Well, if you could call a laughing hyena charming.

BARNABY. A handsome face. *[He tries to look heroic]*

WIDOW PIPER. Is a baboon's face handsome? What else?

BARNABY. I'll soon be filthy rich!

WIDOW PIPER. Well, you're half way there already. You're filthy.

BARNABY. This is serious, madam. I was speaking of marriage.

WIDOW PIPER. And I was saying, "I do, I do." I'll marry you. *[She hugs him tightly]*

BARNABY. What?! *[He pushes her away]* Not you, madam. One of your daughters.

WIDOW PIPER. *[Angrily]* One of my daughters? What's wrong with me?

BARNABY. Madam, I would tell you, but I don't have all day.

WIDOW PIPER. How dare you! *[She pauses]* Just who is it you wish to marry, you old goat?

BARNABY. Your youngest.

WIDOW PIPER. Mistress Mary? Never in a million years!

BARNABY. When I get rich, I'll be willing to pay you well.

WIDOW PIPER. When you get rich, come back and see me. Until then, good day, sir.

BARNABY. Madam, you cannot stop me!

WIDOW PIPER. Oh, no? There's some dirt on your chin.

BARNABY. Where? *[He feels of his chin. WIDOW PIPER gives his elbow an upper cut, slamming his fist into his own chin]* Owwww!

WIDOW PIPER. Do you see who's coming over there? *[She points behind him. He turns around to look]*

BARNABY. Over where?

WIDOW PIPER. Over there! *[As he bends over to look, she kicks him, pushing him toward the other side of the stage. He lands in the arms of GONZORGO and RODERIGO, who have just entered. She dusts off her hands]* The very idea–wanting to marry that sweet young thing when I'm still available. *[She starts into her house, but is met by MARY coming out with two packed bags. BARNABY is too busy to notice]* What is this?

MARY. I'm sorry, Mother Piper. I can't stay here any longer.

WIDOW PIPER. What?

MARY. I'm running off to Toyland, and I may never return! *[She cries and runs off]*

WIDOW PIPER. But, Mistress Mary . . .

GONZORGO. *[Sees Mary]* Say, isn't that Mistress Mary, the girl you want to . . . ?

BARNABY. Please! Don't talk to me about women just now.

RODERIGO. Yeah, but it looks like she's running . . .

BARNABY. *[He turns and indicates the Widow Piper]* That's the Widow Piper. Let her run. *[The WIDOW PIPER exits into her house]*

GONZORGO. *[Shrugs his shoulders]* But the other girl . . .

RODERIGO. She didn't look like any widow I've ever seen.

BARNABY. Well, at least I know now why she's a widow.

GONZORGO. Why's that?

BARNABY. To get away from her, her husband probably jumped off a cliff.

RODERIGO. Jumped off a cliff? *[He begins to cry]* Was he hurt?

BARNABY. Will you stop crying? We've got serious business to transact.

GONZORGO. Yeah, so have we. Our payment. *[He and RODERIGO hold out their hands simultaneously]*

RODERIGO. In cash.

BARNABY. You can put your hands back in your pockets, men. The dastardly deed you deceivers did is undone.

GONZORGO. What are you talking about? You pay us, or we get real mean. Ain't that right, Roderigo?

RODERIGO. Real mean, Gonzorgo. *[They growl]*

BARNABY. I'll pay you for getting rid of Alan—as soon as you get rid of him.

GONZORGO. What are you saying?

BARNABY. That he's still alive.

RODERIGO. That's impossible.

BARNABY. The boat sank in only three feet of water. He got away.

GONZORGO. Hang it, Roderigo. I knew we shoulda moved the ship away from the dock before it sank.

BARNABY. And Alan is preventing me from reaching my two greatest goals.

RODERIGO. And what are they—if I may ask, sir?

Music No. 5: "HE WON'T BE HAPPY TILL HE GETS IT"

BARNABY. First:
Because of Alan's big inheritance, he's filthy rich;
And when I think of all that dough, I get this sudden itch;
Conniving wheels inside my head begin to spin with plans
On how to finish him and get his cash into my hands;

And I won't be happy till I get it;
Just think of all the things that I could buy—
A house upon the hill and every added frill;
Yes, I'm going to get it by and by.

GONZORGO/RODERIGO. And he won't be happy till he gets it;
Just think of all the things that he could buy—

GONZORGO. A house upon the hill . . .
RODERIGO. And every added frill–
ALL THREE. Yes, (I'm/he's) going to get it by and by.
BARNABY. Second:

Well, I want Mistress Mary Quite Contrary as my bride,
And I will have her if she doesn't run somewhere and hide;
I know that she'd be happy with me as a husband true,
If only she could love me half as much as I–do.

And I won't be happy till I get her,
For she's the fairest girl that money can buy;
She may as well consent, 'cause I'm the lucky gent
Who is going to get her by and by.

GONZORGO/RODERIGO. And he won't be happy till he gets her,
For she's the fairest girl that money can buy. . .
GONZORGO. She may as well consent . . .
RODERIGO. 'Cause he's the lucky gent . . .
ALL THREE. Who is going to get her by and by.

GONZORGO. *[Following the song]* What do you want me and Roderigo to do?

BARNABY. Alan is supposed to meet me here in a few minutes to collect his inheritance. I told him you two would lead him to my new home up on the hill.

RODERIGO. But we don't even know where it is.

BARNABY. And you don't need to know. I want you to lead him astray. Take him deep into the woods–and lose him.

GONZORGO. *[Ominously]* But the only woods in Mother Goose County is the Forest of the Giant Spiders!

RODERIGO. People go there alive–and come back dead!

BARNABY. Yes, that's right. Tee-hee-hee.

GONZORGO. But you don't want us to die, do you?

BARNABY. Yes!

RODERIGO. What?

BARNABY. I mean, no. Of course not. *[He grabs Roderigo's shirt front]* But I want Alan dead–no matter what! Do I make myself clear? *[RODERIGO begins to cry loudly]* Will you please stop slobbering on my suit? *[He wipes his jacket as he looks off]* Here he comes. Now, remember what I said. Be sure he never comes out of the Spider Forest alive! Hmmmm? And I'll pay you handsomely. *[Aside]* If you live. *[He exits quickly]* Tee-hee-hee.

RODERIGO. *[As he shakes visibly]* Gonzorgo, d-d-do we really have to go into *that* forest?

GONZORGO. Don't worry, Roderigo. If any spiders attack us, I'll squash them under foot–like this! Grrrrrr! *[He stomps his toe and mashes it into the ground. RODERIGO cries loudly]* What's the matter? Did I frighten you?

RODERIGO. No. That's my toe you're squashing! *[GONZORGO raises his foot. RODERIGO cries in pain]*

GONZORGO. Sorry.

ALAN. *[Enters, looks around, approaches the two men. He looks at them suspiciously]* Do I know you two?

GONZORGO. *[Clumsily trying to disguise his voice]* Not possible. We're, uh, new in town.

ALAN. If you both had long black beards, you would look exactly like the two thugs who abducted me and tried to drown me.

RODERIGO. It wasn't us. It must have been two other thugs.

GONZORGO. Are you Alan?

ALAN. Yes.

RODERIGO. We're to lead you to Mr. Barnaby's new house on the hill. *[He gives a wink to Gonzorgo]*

ALAN. I'm ready.

GONZORGO. *[Points off]* Right this way, then. Up the north road.

ALAN. The north road? But that leads to the Forest of the Giant Spiders.

GONZORGO. *[As he and RODERIGO wink with each other]* It does? Well, how about that?

RODERIGO. *[Tries to laugh]* Yeah. How about that? *[He cries loudly and shakes all over]*

ALAN. Well, if we have to. What are we waiting for? Let's go. *[Exits]*

Music No. 6A: "HE WON'T BE HAPPY TILL HE GETS IT" (reprise)

GONZORGO/RODERIGO. *[They sing with some fear of what lies ahead]* And he won't be happy till he gets it;
Just think of all the things that he could buy–

GONZORGO. A house upon the hill . . .

RODERIGO. And every added frill–

GONZORGO/RODERIGO. *[As they exit after Alan]* Yes, he's going to get it by and by.

[LIGHTS dim to blackout for scene change]

Music No. 6B: "SCENE CHANGE MUSIC" (Segue into . . .)
Music No. 6C: "MYSTERIOUS MUSIC"

Scene 2

[The Spider Forest; a few hours later. It is dark. Large tree branches overhang in an ominous fashion. At one side is a giant spider web strung between the trees.

AT RISE: *A shadowy SPIDER lurks for a few seconds at the web, hears a noise offstage, and slips behind a tree. The Spider is attached to its web by a white cord or length of webbing.*

MISTRESS MARY breaks through the brush with a scream and falls on the ground, dropping her bags, as the MUSIC comes to an end. She gasps for breath. Slowly looking about, she pulls herself to her feet and stumbles this way and that]

MARY. Which way? Which way to Toyland? *[She sighs deeply]* I'm so tired, I really don't care. *[She leans against a tree. The SPIDER peeks around the tree and makes a slurping sound. MARY looks up; the SPIDER hides]* What was that? I'm lost. That's it. I'm totally lost. *[She crosses back toward the tree. The SPIDER comes into view and watches her. It reaches for her, but she moves away]* I should have gone the other way to Toyland, but I thought this shortcut would be quicker. *[She crosses toward the tree again]* And now I don't know where I am. *[She backs unknowingly into the web. It sticks to her]* What . . . ? What is this? *[She tries to pull it off, but she cannot]* It's so sticky, I can't . . . get it off. *[She becomes tied up in the web. The SPIDER steps from behind the tree to watch]* It . . . it feels like a . . . like a spider web. I can't get loose! *[The SPIDER makes its noise. MARY turns to see it]* Yeeeiii! It *is* a spider web! *[She struggles more frantically but cannot break free]* Help! Help me, someone! A giant spider's got me! *[The SPIDER steps toward her, slurping all the time. MARY screams. Just as the SPIDER is about to grab her, ALAN breaks through the underbrush. He pauses to take in the scene]* Alan! Alan, it's you! Help me! Get this spider away from me! *[The SPIDER pauses, turning to see Alan. It makes angry noises as if to frighten him]*

ALAN. Mistress Mary! I don't understand . . . What are you doing . . .?

MARY. This is no time for talk, Alan. Save me from this ugly thing.

ALAN. Right away. *[He picks up a long branch and pokes the spider with it]* Move on, Spider. Leave her alone. Go on. I don't want to hurt you. *[The SPIDER grabs the branch and holds it still. ALAN cannot shake it loose]* Uh-oh! I think *it* wants to hurt *me. [To the Spider]* There's no need to get upset. *[The SPIDER breaks the branch in two]* It's upset. Whoaaaa! *[ALAN runs about the clearing as the SPIDER follows, though at a slower pace. ALAN pulls a knife from his pocket or belt and faces it]* I'll stab you if you come any closer.

MARY. Alan, watch out. You can't get close enough to him.

ALAN. Whoaaa! *[He runs again]* This is getting serious. *[He runs close to Mary and falls]*

MARY. Oh, Alan, you're done for! *[The SPIDER stands over Alan and snarls]* We're both lost!

ALAN. *[As the SPIDER leans over him]* Wait a minute. I know how to stop a spider. Don't go after *it.*

MARY. That's right. Go after its *web.*

ALAN. One web–coming up! *[ALAN picks up the cord that is attached from the web to the spider]* One spider–going down. *[The SPIDER pleads for ALAN not to cut the cord, but he does anyway]* There–your lifeline's gone! So long, Mr. Spider. *[The SPIDER looks helpless, tottering as if losing its balance. It whimpers as it falls backwards and offstage. Its voice fades in the distance]*

MARY. He'll have to build himself another web somewhere else.

ALAN. *[As he cuts Mary free]* But Mistress Mary, what are you doing here?

MARY. I was on my way to Toyland, and I got lost. *[They move to one side of the clearing and talk in mime as GONZORGO and RODERIGO appear at the other side of the clearing]*

GONZORGO. Well, he got away from us again, but we'll find him if it takes all . . .

RODERIGO. *[Seeing Alan over Gonzorgo's shoulder, he waves for Gonzorgo to be quiet and to look at the same time. He whispers]* Unhh. Mmmmmm. Unhhh!

GONZORGO. Huh? What is it? What are you waving about?

RODERIGO. Mnnn! *[He turns GONZORGO so he sees Alan]*

GONZORGO. What is it? It's Alan! Why, I'll rip him . . .

RODERIGO. *[Whispering]* Wait. Isn't that the girl that old Barnaby wants to marry?

GONZORGO. Yeah, it is. We can take the two of them.

RODERIGO. And get two times the reward.

GONZORGO. For once you've had a good idea. Come on. I'll bash *him* and *you* get the girl. *[RODERIGO starts off, but GONZORGO holds him back]* Let's wait for the right moment. Quick–hide. *[They wait in hiding and watch]*

ALAN. Let's get some rest. It will be daylight soon.

Music No. 7: "GO TO SLEEP, SLUMBER DEEP"

MARY. But I'm so frightened. *[Sings]* See that shadow sway?
ALAN. *[Sings]* That is nothing, dear.
MARY. Please don't go away.
ALAN. I am staying here.
MARY. See the creepies crawl?
ALAN. No, that cannot be.
MARY. See that ogre tall?
ALAN. It's a cypress tree.
Go to sleep, slumber deep,
Little one, I'll watch o'er you while you sleep.
MARY. *[Spoken]* Yes, I'll . . . *[Sings]* Dream and rest, that is best
Till I hear the morning song from bough and nest.

[Trying to help Alan and Mary go to sleep, GONZORGO and RODERIGO sneak up near them and join in the singing. They threaten them in mime as the song progresses, but MARY and ALAN are not aware of them. The CHORUS also sings offstage]

ALL. Go to sleep, slumber deep,
Little one(s), we'll watch o'er you while you sleep.
Dream and rest, that is best
Till you hear the morning song from bough and nest.

[GONZORGO and RODERIGO accidentally doze off and snore loudly. MARY and ALAN hear them]

MARY. Somebody's snoring!

ALAN. It's those two scoundrels who have been trying to kill me.

MARY. Let's run. We'll be safe in Toyland.

ALAN. Hurry. We'll lose them. *[They grab Mary's bags and rush off into the woods. The SPIDER enters, snarling and angry. It sees the two men. It waves its arms and growls over them]*

GONZORGO. *[Half asleep]* Stop growling, Roderigo.

RODERIGO. *[The SPIDER snarls again]* I'm not growling, Gonzorgo.

GONZORGO. Well, if you're not growling, and I'm not growling, who's growling?

RODERIGO. *[Sees the Spider]* He is.

GONZORGO. Who is? *[He sees the Spider]* Owwwww, Roderigo,

it's a killer spider! Let's get out of here! *[He jumps up, runs into the web, and gets stuck]* Owwwww!

RODERIGO. *[As he avoids the SPIDER's clutches]* Let's go, let's go! *[He runs offstage. After a pause, he comes back]* Aren't you coming?

GONZORGO. I'm stuck in this stupid web! Help me!

RODERIGO. *[They struggle against the web as the SPIDER grabs one of Gonzorgo's arms]* Let go of the spider, Gonzorgo! *[RODERIGO grabs his other arm and tugs]*

GONZORGO. I'm not holding the spider! The spider's holding me! *[After a battle, RODERIGO pulls GONZORGO free]* Let's get out of here! *[They stumble over each other trying to get away. They finally exit in the same direction Alan and Mary took. The SPIDER chases after them]*

Music No. 8: "MUSIC" (plays to a climax)

BLACKOUT

[An intermission may be taken here, or the action may be continuous]

Alan, Spider, Mary (Theatre U. S. A.)

ACT II

Music No. 9: "MUSIC" (for opening of the curtain)

[If no intermission is taken, Music No. 8 segues into Music No. 9. MUSIC builds No. 9 to a climax as the Toyland scene is revealed on stage: A large, elaborately decorated toyshop. It is a few hours later. A large (neon, if possible) sign saying "TOYLAND" hangs from above. There are entrances Right, Left, and Up Center. Several human-sized dolls of different types stand stiffly about. Traditionally, these are toy soldiers similar to the ones in The Nutcracker Ballet, *though any kinds of dolls may be used.*

At one side, there is a huge, colorful machine large enough for a person to walk through. It has buttons, switches, and colored lights all over it.

AT RISE: *GRUMIO, a young Toyshop apprentice wearing a messy apron, studies the machine closely. TOYMASTER enters carrying a clipboard or blueprints. He is a kindly, older, forgetful man with white hair and a beard, with great energy for his work]*

TOYMASTER. Well, Grumio, what do you think?

GRUMIO. Well, sir, I think . . .

TOYMASTER. *[Admiring the machine]* The Gizmoh! If it works, Grumio, we'll be hailed as the world's greatest toy inventors.

GRUMIO. Well, sir, I think . . .

TOYMASTER. Imagine—bringing plastic and wooden dolls . . . to life!

GRUMIO. Well, sir, I think . . .

TOYMASTER. Come on, boy. Loosen your tongue. What do you think?

GRUMIO. Well, sir . . .

TOYMASTER. Yes? Out with it, Grumio.

GRUMIO. Well, sir, we attached the dumbleglat to the whichnoodle, when we should have screwed the bipdull to the roynose.

TOYMASTER. Nonsense, my boy. The dumbleglat is where it is supposed to be.

GRUMIO. Well, sir, I think . . .

TOYMASTER. Stop thinking, Grumio, and turn the blasted thing on. There's one way to find out for sure.

GRUMIO. Yes, sir. *[He flips a switch]* Wait. We forgot the subject. *[He pushes one of the nearby dolls into the opening in the machine]*

Come on, dolly. You will be our first test. If we can bring you to life, we can give life to all the toys. There. Stay right there.

TOYMASTER. *[He reads from the clipboard or blueprints as GRUMIO turns knobs and slips switches]* Ready? Let me see. We turn on the sitbun, the whonotch, the whipurr, and the jiggabit.

GRUMIO. Got them.

TOYMASTER. Turn the picklepit to eight, the hoocheepoo to sixteen, and the quibblenook to eighty-five. *[He puts on some goggles]*

GRUMIO. Done. *[He puts on his goggles]*

TOYMASTER. And then–boom!–it lights up! *[He gives a flourish, but the machine remains quiet]* It, uh, is supposed to light up, isn't it? Gizmoh, do your thing!

GRUMIO. Well, sir, I think . . .

TOYMASTER. I said, "Gizmoh, do your thing!"

GRUMIO. Well, sir, I think . . .

TOYMASTER. I don't understand it, Grumio. What do you think?

GRUMIO. *[He picks up a huge plug that runs from the machine]* Well, sir, I think we forgot something. *[He shows the plug]* We forgot to plug it in.

TOYMASTER. Oh. Yes. Well, of course. Plug it in. *[GRUMIO does. The machine goes wild, with lights flashing and out-of-this-world noises. The two MEN are very excited. They laugh and slap each other on the back at their success]*

GRUMIO. It's working, it's working! *[The DOLL begins to shake, a little at first, and then violently. Suddenly, there is an explosion. Smoke rises from the machine, its noises run down, and the DOLL jerks into an awkward, rigid position with its hair standing on end. They blow and fan the smoke away]*

TOYMASTER. Grumio? *[He takes his goggles off]*

GRUMIO. Yes, sir? *[He removes his goggles]*

TOYMASTER. I think you had better turn the Gizmoh off.

GRUMIO. Yes, sir. *[He does]* Does this mean that we will go back to making normal toys, sir?

TOYMASTER. I'm afraid so, my boy. If we didn't make them, no children would have any toys for Christmas. And that wouldn't do, would it?

GRUMIO. No, sir. *[Pause as he thinks]* Still, if we had attached the bipdull to the roynose . . .

TOYMASTER. Forget it, Grumio. We failed to bring our toys to life today. We'll have other opportunities later. Right now, we need to return to our other, more pressing duties. *[He hangs his clipboard or blueprints on the Gizmoh]*

GRUMIO. *[Unhappily]* Yes, sir.

TOYMASTER. Go tell the assembly line people to speed up work on the Ballerina Doll. It's due to be shipped out today.

GRUMIO. Yes, sir. And what about the Drum Major Doll?

TOYMASTER. Bring it in here. I'll work on it myself.

GRUMIO. Yes, sir.

[ALAN and MARY break into the room, rush past the Toymaster and Grumio, and hide. The latter two look at each other questioningly]

TOYMASTER. Who was that, Grumio?

GRUMIO. I don't know, sir. New dolls off the assembly line? *[ALAN and MARY return to Grumio, looking carefully about]*

ALAN/MARY. Shhhh.

GRUMIO. *[To the Toymaster]* Shhhh.

TOYMASTER. Why are you shushing me, Grumio?

GRUMIO. I don't know, sir. *[To Alan and Mary]* Why are you shushing us?

ALAN. Please, don't tell anyone we're here.

MARY. Our lives depend on it.

ALAN/MARY. Shhhh. *[They hide again]*

GRUMIO. *[To the Toymaster]* They said their lives depend . . .

TOYMASTER. I heard what they said, Grumio. *[Kindly, to Alan and Mary]* Come here, my children. *[ALAN and MARY step into view]* Come. You're safe here. *[Pause]* I promise.

ALAN. *[As they cautiously approach him]* Who . . . who are you?

GRUMIO. Why, everybody knows him. He's the Toymaster!

MARY. The Toymaster? Then we made it. We're safe, Alan.

GRUMIO. And I'm Grumio, his apprentice.

ALAN. *[Ignoring Grumio]* Mr. Toymaster, sir, my Uncle Barnaby is trying to kill me to get my inheritance.

GRUMIO. I said, I'm Grumio, his appre–

MARY. *[Ignoring Grumio]* And he's trying to force me to marry him, but I love Alan.

GRUMIO. I'm Grumio . . .

ALAN. Can you help us, sir?

MARY. This is the worst day of my life.

GRUMIO. *[Shakes hands with an imaginary person]* Glad to meet you.

Music No. 10: "TOYLAND"

TOYMASTER. *[In a fatherly way]* Now, now, children. You needn't be worried. You're in Toyland now. I'll protect you. *[MUSIC up]* And, as for this being the worst day of your life, think again, my dear. *[Sings]*

When you've grown up, my dears,
   And are as old as I,
You'll often ponder on the years
   That roll so swiftly by, my dears,
That roll so swiftly by;

And of the many lands
   You will have journeyed through,
You'll oft recall the best of all,
   The land your childhood knew,
Your childhood knew;

Toyland, Toyland,
   Little girl and boy land;
While you dwell within it,
   You are ever happy then;

Childhood's joyland,
   Mystic, merry Toyland;
Once you pass its borders,
   You can never return again.

[All the DOLLS onstage turn toward the audience mechanically and join in the next chorus. An offstage CHORUS might also sing]

ALL. *[Except ALAN and MARY, who watch and listen in awe]*

Toyland, Toyland,
   Little girl and boy land;
While you dwell within it,
   You are ever happy then;

Childhood's joyland,
   Mystic, merry Toyland;
Once you pass its borders,
   You can never return again.

[The DOLLS turn back to their original positions]

TOYMASTER. So, you see, children, as long as you are in Toyland, you are perfectly safe. Grumio, take care of them. See that they have food and drink, and show them to some comfortable rooms. *[To Alan and Mary]* You will have to excuse me. I have lots of work to do. *[He stops by the Doll in the Gizmoh]* I guess I had better take this sizzled doll with me. I'll need to make a few repairs on it. *[He picks up the Doll and carries it off, or pushes it off]*

GRUMIO. I'm Grumio.

ALAN. I'm Alan. And this is my friend, Mistress Mary, Quite Contrary.

GRUMIO. How do you like it here in Toyland?

MARY. *[As she looks around the room]* It . . . it's lovely. Do you really make toy dolls here?

GRUMIO. *[Proudly]* All the toy dolls in the world.

ALAN. What does the song mean when it says, "Toyland–once you pass its borders, you can never return again"?

GRUMIO. It means you'll spend the rest of your days here, of course.

MARY. What? But we don't want to stay. We just want a temporary refuge.

GRUMIO. It's too late for that. No one ever leaves Toyland.

MARY. *[As she rushes into Alan's arms]* Oh, no! We escape from one problem only to run into another.

ALAN. Don't worry, Mistress Mary. We'll find a way out.

GRUMIO. A way out? Why do you want a way out? You just arrived. We're actually very friendly here. *[He indicates the dolls in the room]* And we have all kinds of dolls to play with.

MARY. It's not that, Grumio. We love Mother Goose County. We only left to save ourselves from Barnaby's clutches.

ALAN. We must go back. Will you help us?

GRUMIO. Me? But, I . . . I . . . *[A smile comes over his face]* Sure. Sure, I'll help you. It might even be exciting. But you can't leave on any of the roads. They're all guarded. We'll have to think up a new way. *[He thinks hard]* A new way, a new way. Let me think.

TOYMASTER. *[Enters]* Grumio, did you remember about the Ballerina and the Drum Major Dolls?

GRUMIO. Oh, no, sir. I think . . .

TOYMASTER. Time to stop thinking and get to it, son. *[He exits]*

GRUMIO. Yes, sir. I will, sir. Right away, sir. *[He starts off, but stops]* The Ballerina Doll? And the Drum Major Doll? That's it! That's it! I've got it. Come on, follow me.

MARY. You have an idea?

GRUMIO. The perfect idea! *[They exit excitedly]*

[After a few seconds, RODERIGO appears from Left, looks around at the dolls]

RODERIGO. I love toys.

GONZORGO. *[Appears at Right]* Yessiree, what a layout.

BARNABY. *[Appears Up Center]* Hmmmm, tee-hee-hee. *[GONZORGO waves at BARNABY, who waves back. RODERIGO waves at BARNABY, who waves back. GONZORGO and RODERIGO both wave at BARNABY, who waves back. Then BARNABY comes to his senses]* Will you stop waving at me?! We're not here to play games. *[They gather at Center]* We're here to steal things!

GONZORGO. Yeah!

BARNABY. To destroy property!

GONZORGO. Yeah!

BARNABY. And to *crunch* people! *[He stomps Roderigo's foot. RODERIGO cries]* Now, what's the matter with you? Going soft on us?

RODERIGO. No. You're not crunching people; you're crunching my toeseez.

BARNABY. *[Sarcastically]* Well, do you want me to kiss them for you?

RODERIGO. Will you, please?

BARNABY. *[Exploding]* No, I will not! Just keep them out of my way! *[Pause. In a gruff voice]* Now, you two are sure my nephew Alan and . . . *[in a sugary tone]* my fiancee Mistress Mary. . . *[in a secretive tone]* came here to Toyland?

GONZORGO. Aye, sir. We overheard 'em talking about it.

RODERIGO. Just before we sang them to sleep.

BARNABY. You sang them to sleep?

GONZORGO. Well, actually, we sang us to sleep.

RODERIGO. Just before the giant spider attacked us.

BARNABY. A giant spider attacked you?

GONZORGO. Yeah, but we showed it a thing or two, didn't we, Roderigo?

RODERIGO. Yeah. We showed it how fast we could run. *[They demonstrate]*

MARMADUKE. *[He is an Inspector of the Toyland Police. His costume should be an elaborate and colorful doll version of a policeman.*

He watches them from a hiding place. Then he leaps in front of them and holds out a truncheon] Who goes there?

BARNABY. Who goes where?

MARMADUKE. Huh? Well, I don't know. I've never been asked that question before.

GONZORGO. It's just us, friend. *[He grabs the truncheon and bends it with his bare hands. He hands it back]* Wanna make something of it?

MARMADUKE. Uh, uh, why, no. I was just wondering.

BARNABY. Are you some sort of police officer?

MARMADUKE. Inspector Marmaduke. *[He jerks to attention, banging his head with the truncheon]* Oww! Uh, of the Toyland Police. At your service. A totally dedicated, scrupulously honest, upholder of the law.

GONZORGO. Police? *[Secretly, to Roderigo]* I'll get him from this side, Roderigo. You go around to the other side.

RODERIGO. Ready, set . . .

BARNABY. Wait! *[GONZORGO and RODERIGO fall over each other trying to halt their forward movement]* Exactly how honest are you? *[He flips through a wad of cash]*

MARMADUKE. *[He tries to grab one of the bills. BARNABY slaps his hand]* Oh! Well, about a hundred dollars honest.

BARNABY. Well, here's a hundred and one dollars. *[He hands it to MARMADUKE, who counts it carefully]* Now, we're looking for a pretty young girl named Mistress Mary and a rotten young boy named Alan, who, uh, *kidnapped* her. I'll give you another hundred dollars for the girl, and another hundred if the boy, uh, disappears . . . forever. Tee-hee-hee. Do you get my drift?

MARMADUKE. Consider her found–and him lost. *[Pause]* By the way. . . how will I recognize them?

BARNABY. Do I have to tell you everything? Just look for two strangers in Toyland, and that's them.

MARMADUKE. Oh. Then your problems are over.

BARNABY. Excellent. You mean you've found them already?

MARMADUKE. Certainly. There are two strangers standing right there. *[He points to Gonzorgo and Roderigo]*

BARNABY. What? These two men?

MARMADUKE. They look like strangers to me.

GONZORGO. I'm not a stranger, idiot!

RODERIGO. That's right. I know him very well.

MARMADUKE. Oh. Sorry.

BARNABY. Will you get on with the search? It's very important that my mission be completed shortly.

MARMADUKE. Don't worry, sir. If there are two strangers here in Toyland, I'll find them. *[He takes out a flashlight and shines it around]* Now, let's see. Where could they be? *[He shines the light under Barnaby's cape, and then goes under it and all the way around Barnaby]* Nope, they're not hiding in there.

BARNABY. I know they're not under my cape! Will you look elsewhere?

MARMADUKE. Certainly, sir. What if I look over here? Do you think they might be over here?

BARNABY. Yes, yes. Now, go on–look–before I lose my patience.

MARMADUKE. Don't worry, sir. If you can lose it, Inspector Marmaduke can find it. *[He crosses offstage]* Come here, Alan and Mistress Mary. Inspector Marmaduke just wants to speak to you, that's all.

GONZORGO. I don't think I'd trust him, Mr. Barnaby. He doesn't seem too bright.

BARNABY. Do you know why he doesn't seem too bright, Gonzorgo?

GONZORGO. No, why?

BARNABY. Because he's too much like you, that's why! We had better come up with a plan of our own.

RODERIGO. *[Brightly, child-like]* Oh, I have a plan.

GONZORGO. You have? Well, out with it, Roderigo. What's your plan?

RODERIGO. My plan is we go home.

GONZORGO. Go home? Are you crazy?

RODERIGO. *[He starts to cry]* Oh, Gonzorgo, you don't like any of my plans.

BARNABY. Do I have to listen to this crybaby again? Hmmmm?

GONZORGO. *[Takes Roderigo aside]* Roderigo, stop crying. You're making Mr. Barnaby nervous.

RODERIGO. But we were happy with the carnival, weren't we–before he said he would pay us to drown that poor boy, Alan?

GONZORGO. Yes, but he's going to make us rich. Don't you understand?

RODERIGO. I want to go home.

GONZORGO. All right, look. A few more hours. If we haven't gotten rich by then, it's back to the carnival. Agreed?

RODERIGO. *[Happily]* Agreed. *[They shake hands. MARMADUKE enters and crosses to Barnaby]*

MARMADUKE. All the available evidence indicates that the missing children are not in this room, sir.

BARNABY. *[Angrily]* I know they're not in this room, Inspector. I can *see* they're not in this room.

MARMADUKE. You're very observant, sir.

Music No. 11: "HE WON'T BE HAPPY TILL HE GETS IT" (reprise)

BARNABY. Yes, yes. Now, here is what I want you to do. *[Sings]*
Find the missing girl and bring her to me so that we can wed,
And drag the cursed boy in here so I can bash his head;
If you can carry out this villainy swiftly and with dash,
Then you will have my thanks and I'll have pockets full of cash.

And I won't be happy till I get it;
Just think of all the things that I could buy–
A bunch of dirty slobs to do my dirty jobs;
And I'm going to get it by and by.

GONZORGO/RODERIGO/MARMADUKE. And he won't be happy till he gets it;
Just think of all the things that he could buy–

GONZORGO. A bunch of dirty slobs

RODERIGO. To do his dirty jobs;

ALL FOUR. And (I'm/he's) going to get it by and by.

MARMADUKE. *[After the song]* Since I've eliminated this room as a haven for the subjects, I'll check the workshop next. There are a lot of good hiding places in there. *[He exits, continuing to flash his light around]*

GONZORGO. Now, Mr. Barnaby, what next?

BARNABY. Next, we think. *[He gets into a thinking position and walks a few steps and stops]*

GONZORGO. Next, we think. *[He and RODERIGO imitate Barnaby]*

BARNABY. Something will come to us. *[He walks a few more paces]*

RODERIGO. Something will come to us. *[They imitate Barnaby]*

BARNABY. A plan, a plan. *[He walks again]*

GONZORGO. A plan, a plan. *[They imitate Barnaby]*

BARNABY. *[Sees what they are doing]* WILL YOU STOP THAT! *[GONZORGO and RODERIGO stop suddenly]* Walk this way. *[He gestures and walks Offstage Right]*

RODERIGO. Walk this way. *[He gestures the same way and they exit Right imitating Barnaby]*

[After a few seconds, GRUMIO enters Left, looks over the scene, then calls off Left]

GRUMIO. The coast is clear. Come on. Mistress Mary?

MARY. *[She enters dressed as a Ballerina]* But, Grumio, do you really think this disguise will work?

GRUMIO. Being a Ballerina Doll may keep you from being spotted by your suitor.

MARY. But I'm afraid I never learned to dance on toe. *[She tries, but fails]* See?

GRUMIO. *[Calls off Left]* Alan?

ALAN. *[He enters dressed as a Drum Major carrying a baton]* Do I have to wear this?

GRUMIO. You make a fine Drum Major Doll. Besides, this way, we can ship you out of Toyland just like we ship the dolls.

TOYMASTER. *[From off Left]* Grumio? Grumio, come here this instant.

GRUMIO. Yes, sir. I'm on my way, sir. *[To Alan]* It's the Toymaster. Excuse me a minute. *[Starts off; returns]* And remember–while I'm gone, you two are dolls–wooden dolls. *[He exits Left]*

MARY. Oh, Alan, I'm so frightened. Do you think we'll ever be safe again?

ALAN. Mistress Mary, we'll be fine as long as we remain calm.

GONZORGO. *[From Offstage Right]* I'll look over here, Roderigo.

ALAN/MARY. Gonzorgo! *[They freeze in doll-like positions]*

GONZORGO. *[Enters and looks around quickly. He pauses at Mary and Alan]* Hmmmm, I don't remember seeing these dolls before. *[After a short pause, he exits Left]*

MARY. *[As she and ALAN gasp for breath]* What a close call! I couldn't have held my breath a second longer.

RODERIGO. *[From Offstage Right]* Gonzorgo, which way did you go?

ALAN/MARY. Roderigo! *[They freeze in different positions]*

RODERIGO. *[Enters Right and looks around quickly. He pauses at Alan and Mary]* Gee, I'd love to have two dolls like those. *[Pause]* They look awfully familiar. *[He pauses again before exiting Left]*

MARY. *[As they pant again]* I thought he recognized us.

ALAN. But he didn't. That's what counts.

MARMADUKE. *[He enters Up Center, still waving his flashlight around]* Who's there? *[He studies the frozen "dolls" a few seconds]* Strange things are going on in Toyland today.

BARNABY. *[From offstage]* Gonzorgo? Roderigo? Where are you?

ALAN/MARY/MARMADUKE. Barnaby! *[All three freeze in different doll-like positions. BARNABY enters Right, while his two MEN enter Left. They meet at Center, on both sides of ALAN and MARY, who are terrified, and MARMADUKE. All three notice the "dolls" and circle them]*

GONZORGO. Wait. Just a few minutes ago this doll was posed like this. *[He imitates Alan's first pose]*

RODERIGO. No, he was posed like this. *[He imitates Alan's second pose]*

GONZORGO. *[Points to Marmaduke]* And that one wasn't even here.

RODERIGO. Yes, it was–I think.

GONZORGO. No, it wasn't!

BARNABY. Will you two stop playing with the dolls and report on your progress? Have you found Alan and Mistress Mary?

GONZORGO. No, sir. *[He places his arm on Alan's shoulder]* But I've got a feeling they're real close.

RODERIGO. Have you come up with a devious plan?

BARNABY. *[Picks up the clipboard from the Gizmoh]* No, but I feel like it's right under my hands. *[Reads the plans]* Hmmmm! *[Bigger]* Ohhhh!! *[Biggest]* AHHHH!!!

RODERIGO. *[As he studies the "dolls" closely]* Gonzorgo, I think this doll is breathing.

GONZORGO. Don't be stupid.

BARNABY. *[Points wildly to Roderigo]* This is it! The Toymaster has been working on a plan to breathe life into his dolls.

RODERIGO. Well, he doesn't have to breathe life into this one, because it's already breathing.

GONZORGO. *[To Barnaby]* Yeah? So?

BARNABY. *[Points to the Gizmoh]* This must be the machine that does it.

MARMADUKE. *[As he breaks his freeze for a second]* Clever man.

RODERIGO. *[To Barnaby]* Gee, live dolls!

BARNABY. *[Being devilish]* But suppose, just suppose, that the wires got crossed in just the wrong way. Hmmmm?

GONZORGO. *[Gleefully]* Yeah. Just suppose.

RODERIGO. Why? What would happen then?

GONZORGO. Roderigo, don't you know anything? *[He thinks. To Barnaby]* Uh, what would happen then?

BARNABY. All the dolls would become . . . killers! They would turn on all the children.

GONZORGO. It would be chaos!

RODERIGO. *[He cannot believe the thought]* Mean dolls? I've never heard of mean dolls. Dolls are supposed to be good, not mean.

BARNABY. Don't you see? This is our way to become rich and famous. We'll turn the dolls into evil creatures. They'll find and kill Alan. I'll get his inheritance and wed Mistress Mary. Then we can direct the dolls to kill others so we can steal their money too. It's a great plan! Tee-hee-hee!

GONZORGO. And Roderigo and I get rich, too–right?

RODERIGO. Gee, I don't know, Gonzorgo. Mean dolls?

BARNABY. *[As he glances at the papers]* But we've got to have more information that this. We need . . . the Toymaster! Tee-hee-hee! Come along, you scurvy rascals. It's time you did some work. *[BARNABY exits Right with GONZORGO following. RODERIGO stays behind to examine the "dolls" and to show his reluctance to join the plan. GONZORGO returns and grabs Roderigo]*

GONZORGO. Let's go, Roderigo.

RODERIGO. But I tell you that doll is breathing! *[GONZORGO pulls him off]*

GONZORGO. Dolls do not breathe!

MARMADUKE. *[Follows them unseen to the door]* I had better follow up on these brilliant new clues. *[He tiptoes after them]*

MARY. *[Indicating Marmaduke]* Who was that?

TOYMASTER. *[From offstage]* Grumio, what did you do with the Ballerina Doll's clothes?

ALAN. Uh-oh. More trouble. *[He and MARY freeze in doll-like positions again]*

TOYMASTER. *[As he enters Left]* Well, here they are right here. *[GRUMIO rushes to Mary and tries to hide her with his body]* Why did you take this costume off the other doll and put it on this one?

GRUMIO. Well, I, uh . . .

TOYMASTER. Strip her immediately.

MARY. What?!

TOYMASTER. *[As he looks closely at Grumio]* Has your voice changed?

GRUMIO. *[He tries to make it sound like Mary's]* Uh, no, sir. It's just a frog in my throat.

TOYMASTER. Very well, then. Strip this doll at once.

GRUMIO. You mean . . . you mean, take its clothes off?

TOYMASTER. Certainly. And put them back on the other doll. *[As GRUMIO hesitates, the TOYMASTER looks over Alan. GRUMIO rushes to stand in front of Alan]* Oh, my, what a horrible piece of workmanship.

ALAN. I beg your pardon?

TOYMASTER. *[Looks at Alan and then at Grumio]* Still having trouble with your throat, Grumio?

GRUMIO. *[He tries to sound like Alan]* Uh, yes, sir. Sorry, sir.

TOYMASTER. *[He pushes Grumio aside as he studies Alan]* Ah, the face was poorly carved. The nose sticks out too far, the ears are lopsided, and the eyes don't look real enough. Remind me to fire the person who carved this one.

GRUMIO. Uh, yes, sir.

TOYMASTER. *[Indicating Mary]* Haven't you stripped that one yet, Grumio?

GRUMIO. *[As he dances around Mary trying to decide what to do]* Well, I, uh . . . well, uh . . .

TOYMASTER. Wait. *[Crosses to Alan]* Let's do this one first.

GRUMIO. *[Relieved]* Oh, yes, sir. Let's. *[In unison, he and MARY both wipe perspiration from their foreheads]*

TOYMASTER. Get me a hammer and nails. I need to attach this medal to his chest.

ALAN. A hammer and nails?!

TOYMASTER. *[Does a take]* Yes. Now, go on. *[GRUMIO gets them, as the TOYMASTER studies Alan's chest]* I'll put it right about . . . here. Yes, that should look nice. *[GRUMIO hands him the hammer and nails. Then he turns away and cringes]* Two nails should do it. *[ALAN begins to shake wildly]* Grumio, I think this doll is shaking.

GRUMIO. Well, I would to, if you were going to hammer some nails into *my* chest.

ALAN. Whooaaa! *[He runs to Mary]*

TOYMASTER. What? Why, this is no . . . !

BARNABY. *[Appears at the side and points toward the Toymaster]* There he is, men! Grab him!

GONZORGO. *[Growls loudly as he and RODERIGO grab Grumio]* Grrrrr!

RODERIGO. Gotcha, Mr. Toymaster.

ALAN. *[Secretly to Mary]* We're done for now.

MARY. Hold your position.

GRUMIO. Toymaster? I'm not the Toymaster.

GONZORGO. Then who's the Toymaster?

BARNABY. *[Points to him]* That's the Toymaster, you fools. *[They throw Grumio aside and growl loudly as they grab the Toymaster]*

RODERIGO. Gotcha, Mr. Toymaster. *[Pause]* You *are* the Toymaster, aren't you?

TOYMASTER. What is the meaning of this outrage? Unhand me at once. *[GONZORGO and RODERIGO release him]*

BARNABY. Take him in hand. *[They do]*

TOYMASTER. Release me, I say. *[They do]*

BARNABY. Who is paying you–him or me? Hmmmm? *[They grab the Toymaster again]*

TOYMASTER. What do you want from me, you cruel fiend?

BARNABY. *[As fiendishly as possible]* The secret to your life-giving machine. Hmmmm? *[He holds up the plans]*

TOYMASTER. I'll never give you the secret. That kind of knowledge in the wrong hands could be devastating to the entire world!

BARNABY. Yes! And that is exactly why I want it–to devastate the entire world. Tee-hee-hee.

TOYMASTER. My lips are sealed.

BARNABY. But not for long. Roderigo, hurt him. *[RODERIGO pinches the Toymaster lightly]*

TOYMASTER. Ow.

BARNABY. Hurt him worse than that. *[RODERIGO slaps him lightly across the chest]* That didn't hurt him. I said hurt him!

GONZORGO. Leave it to me, captain. *[He twists the Toymaster's arm behind him]*

TOYMASTER. *[Who is now genuinely hurt]* Owwwww!

BARNABY. More, Gonzorgo. *[He does. TOYMASTER falls to the floor in pain]*

TOYMASTER. Owwwwwwwww! Please, I can't take much more of this.

BARNABY. Gonzorgo? One more time. *[As GONZORGO starts to twist his arm again, GRUMIO speaks up]*

GRUMIO. Wait! *[BARNABY signals for GONZORGO to halt]* I'll give you the secret.

BARNABY. *[As he rubs his hands in delight]* Excellent. Now, we're getting somewhere. Hmmmm? *[To Grumio]* All right, kid. Fix the machine. *[GRUMIO reluctantly plugs it in. It lights up and begins to whir]*

MARY. *[Secretly to Alan]* Alan, isn't there anything we can do?

ALAN. I'm thinking, Mistress Mary. I'm thinking.

BARNABY. Beautiful, beautiful!

GRUMIO. *[Still reluctantly]* Last time we tried it, the Doll was destroyed. I think that was because we needed to attach the bipdull to the roynose, instead of . . .

BARNABY. Never mind all that. Just do it.

GRUMIO. Yes, sir. *[He replugs two wires]* There. I think it's ready.

BARNABY. *[He reads from the plans]* Fine. Turn on the sitbun, the whonotch, the whipurr, and the jiggabit.

GRUMIO. *[As he does it]* Done.

BARNABY. And now . . . *[He pushes Grumio out of the way and picks up two sets of plugged cables]* What happens if I cross these two cables?

TOYMASTER. *[Frightened]* You can't do that! That . . . that would make all the dolls evil. They might even . . . kill.

BARNABY. Really? *[He smiles and laughs]* Excellent. *[He unplugs, crosses the wires, and replugs]* There. Watch, Gonzorgo, Roderigo. We're making evil happen! Turn it on, kid. *[GRUMIO does. Flashing lights and various sounds occur]* Now, bring on the Dolls. Start with those two. *[He points to Alan and Mary]*

Music No. 12: "THE MARCH OF THE TOYS"

[One by one, the DOLLS, beginning with ALAN and MARY, are placed in the machine. As each stands under it, BARNABY pulls a big lever that shines a light or lets out a puff of smoke, or produces some other appropriate effect. Each DOLL then is jolted into life, moves stiffly in time to the music, and joins the march around the stage]

BARNABY. Kill, you stupid dolls—kill!

GONZORGO. Kill them! *[He points to the Toymaster and Grumio]*

BARNABY/GONZORGO. Kill, kill, kill! *[At their command, the DOLLS become vicious. At the same time, though, MARMADUKE sneaks onstage and switches the plugs back to the way they originally were. The Gizmoh begins to make a new kind of noise to indicate its sudden change]*

[As BARNABY and GONZORGO laugh, the DOLLS turn toward them and attack them in dance. BARNABY, GONZORGO, and RODERIGO end up crumpled on the floor. Near the end of the Music, the DOLLS exit, leaving the bad guys defeated. MARMADUKE crosses to them, places a foot on Barnaby, and raises his hat triumphantly. After the number, ALAN and MARY break their disguises and run to Marmaduke]

ALAN. We . . . we thought you were on their side.

MARMADUKE. Inspector Marmaduke of the Toyland Police Department is a totally dedicated, scrupulously honest, upholder of the law.

TOYMASTER. And we owe him a vote of thanks. It was he who changed the wiring so the Dolls would attack these ruffians rather than the rest of us. *[He crosses to the Gizmoh and moves some dials]*

BARNABY. Mistress Mary, does this mean our wedding is off?

TOYMASTER. Take them away, Inspector. Let the Toyland judge deal with them.

ALAN. This means that I will get my inheritance at long last.

MARY. And we will be free to wed.

TOYMASTER. Remember, children, you are always welcome—and safe—in Toyland.

GRUMIO. *[As he turns the Gizmoh back on]* Just think, sir, the Gizmoh really brought the Dolls to life this time. It really works. *[He quickly shoves a remaining DOLL into the machine]*

TOYMASTER. I wouldn't do that, if I were you, Grumio.

GRUMIO. Just one Doll—for a test.

TOYMASTER. You shouldn't. *[GRUMIO turns the machine on. It acts as it did before—lots of noise, smoking, and flashing lights]*

GRUMIO. No, it works, it works!

TOYMASTER. I don't want the machine to be misused ever again. So I set it on . . . self-destruct! *[It blows up. There is lots of smoke. When it clears, GRUMIO comes out of the smoke with torn clothing and a soot-covered face]*

GRUMIO. Sir, I think I like the Dolls just like they are. Don't you? *[They laugh. BLACKOUT]*

The **CURTAIN** falls, then re-opens for Curtain Calls

Music No. 13A: Intro to "TOYLAND" for Curtain Calls

[As the CURTAIN rises for the Curtain Calls, everyone except BARNABY, GONZORGO, RODERIGO, and MARMADUKE enter and sing. The TOY DOLLS sing and move stiffly in character]

Music No. 13B: "TOYLAND"

ALL. *[Faster than before]* Toyland, Toyland, little girl and boy land;
While you dwell within it, you are ever happy then;
Childhood's joyland, mystic, merry Toyland;
Once you pass its borders, you can never return again.

Music No. 13C: Segue to "HE WON'T BE HAPPY TILL HE GETS IT"

[GONZORGO, RODERIGO, and BARNABY enter dressed in prison black-and-white striped shirts, chained together and pulling balls and chains. MARMADUKE enters behind them directing them to jail]

MARMADUKE. *[Sings]* And I won't be happy till they get it;
Just now before the court they caused a row . . .
BARNABY/GONZORGO/RODERIGO. *[Sing]* The judge allowed no bail.
MARMADUKE. It's twenty years in jail . . .
ALL FOUR. And (they're/we're) going to get it starting now. *[They exit]*

Music No. 13D: Segue to "TOYLAND"

ALL. Toyland, Toyland, little girl and boy land;
While you dwell within it, you are ever happy then;
Childhood's joyland, mystic, merry Toyland,
Once you pass its borders, you can never return again.

BLACKOUT

THE CURTAIN FALLS

PRODUCTION NOTES

Props

ACT I, Scene 1

Large Christmas tree (optional—see p. 41)—Mother Goose Chorus
Christmas tree decorations (optional—see p. 41)—Mother Goose Chorus
Miscellaneous props typical of the Mother Goose character (crook for Bo-Peep, pail for Jack and Jill, bowl of curds and whey with spoon for Miss Muffet, lamb on wagon for Mary-Had-a-Little-Lamb, pig for Tom-Tom, bugle or trumpet for Little Boy Blue, etc.)
Giant handkerchief—Roderigo
Slip of paper (bill)—Gonzorgo
Bouquet of flowers with note attached—Barnaby
Similar bouquet, broken and smashed—Barnaby
Tambourines and handbells—Gypsy Chorus
Schoolbooks, slates, chalk—Mother Goose Chorus
2 travelling bags—Mary

ACT I, Scene 2

Tree branch—Alan
Knife—Alan

ACT II

Clipboard or blueprints—Toymaster
Goggles—Toymaster, Grumio
Truncheon—Marmaduke
Wad of paper money—Barnaby
Flashlight—Marmaduke
Drum major's baton—Alan
Shackles, prison balls (styrofoam perhaps), and chains—Barnaby, Roderigo, Gonzorgo

Costumes

Traditional Mother Goose costumes are recommended. Perhaps the opening scene can look like an illustration in a nursery rhyme book.

Special costumes are noted in the stage directions, such as a bandage on **Jack**'s head (Jack and Jill) and a burned spot on **Jack-Be-Nimble**'s seat. **Barnaby** may wear villain black—suit, cape, top hat. The text suggests a shirt (or coveralls) with prison stripes for the curtain call. **Gonzorgo** and **Roderigo** may also wear prison stripes for the curtain call.

For his first entrance **Alan** wears a gypsy woman's dress, with a kerchief covering his hair. In Toyland he puts on a toy drum major's costume. **Mistress Mary** puts on a ballerina doll costume in Toyland.

The script calls for **Grumio** to appear in tattered, soot-covered clothes at the end of the play. He can achieve a quick costume change by underdressing the tattered garments.

(See Floor Plan next page)

Floor Plans

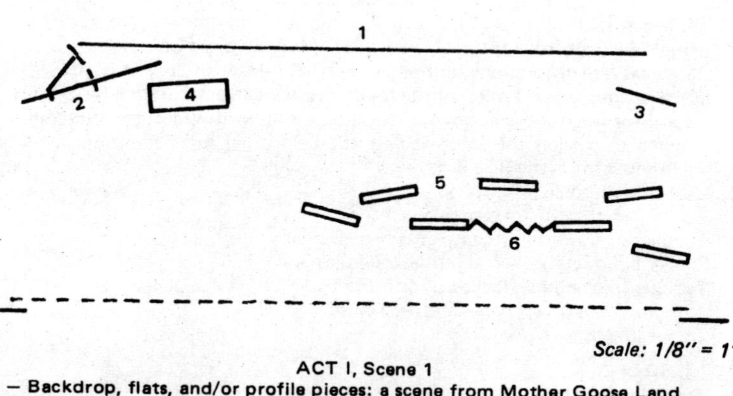

Scale: 1/8" = 1'

ACT I, Scene 1

1 – Backdrop, flats, and/or profile pieces: a scene from Mother Goose Land
2 – Mistress Mary's house, with practical door
3 – A house, or a tree, or trellis of flowers, etc. (to balance stage and permit entrances from behind it)
4 – Bench

Add other decorations, flowers, trees, benches, stools, etc. as desired

ACT I, Scene 2

5 – A grove of trees (may be dropped in front of Mother Goose Land set)
6 – Huge spider web suspended between two trees

ACT II – Toyland

1 – The Gizmoh (videotape of a performance by a university theatre, available from the publisher, shows the Gizmoh working)
2 – Walls of the toyshop

ALTERNATE LYRICS FOR OPENING SONG

(for a non-Christmas presentation)

Music No. 2: "HAIL TO SPRINGTIME"

CHORUS. Hail to Springtime, joyous Springtime–
Hooray! Warm days are near;
Hail to Springtime, joyous Springtime–
Be happy, it's almost here.

Springtime birds sing, waking bees sting,
The sun explodes with light;
Springtime rains fall, and the flowers sprawl,
All making the world so bright.

SOLO. Folks come from Toyland
And from far, far and near;
Folks come to join us
And to share our carnival cheer.

CHORUS. To our fair, to our fair,
They come from miles around for fun and games
At our fair.

Springtime birds sing, waking bees sting,
The sun explodes with light;
Springtime rains fall, and the flowers sprawl,
All making the world so bright.

[MISTRESS MARY makes a grand entrance]

Theatre U. S. A. cast and set